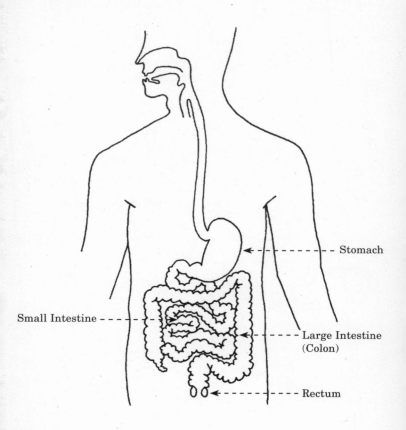

Stomach

Small Intestine

Large Intestine
(Colon)

Rectum

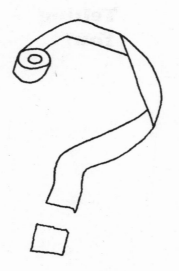

What's Your Poo Telling You?

What's Your Poo Telling You?

Josh Richman and Anish Sheth, M.D.

Illustrations by Peter Arkle

EBURY
PRESS

3 5 7 9 10 8 6 4 2

This edition published 2013
First published in 2007 as *The Book of Poo* by Ebury Press, an imprint of
Ebury Publishing
A Random House Group company
First published in USA by Chronicle Books in 2007

Copyright © Josh Richman and Dr Anish Sheth 2007

Illustrations © Peter Arkle 2007

Josh Richman and Dr Anish Sheth have asserted their right to be
identified as the author of this Work in accordance with the Copyright,
Designs and Patents Act 1988

The Random House Group Limited Reg. No. 954009

Addresses for companies within the Random House Group can
be found at: www.randomhouse.co.uk

A CIP catalogue record for this book is available from the British Library

The Random House Group Limited supports the Forest Stewardship
Council® (FSC®), the leading international forest-certification
organisation. Our books carrying the FSC label are printed on
FSC®-certified paper. FSC is the only forest-certification scheme
supported by the leading environmental organisations, including
Greenpeace. Our paper procurement policy can be found at:
www.randomhouse.co.uk/environment

Printed and bound by CPI Group (UK) Ltd, Croydon, CR0 4YY

ISBN 9780091955557

To buy books by your favourite authors and register for offers visit
www.randomhouse.co.uk

Acknowledgments

In the course of writing this book we realized how many of our friends and family enjoy discussing poo in great detail. Particular thanks go to Ben, Chad, Ross, John, Katie, Simran, and Craig for sharing their personal passions for poo.

To Daniel and Jay, for helping turn a quirky idea into this book.

To Rohan, for providing endless inspiration.

Most of all, special gratitude to our wives, Heather and Shilpa, for appreciating our unique sense of humor.

CONTENTS

Introduction

Not unlike a snowflake, each bowel movement has a uniqueness that should be regarded with wondrous appreciation. Too often dismissed as useless and malodorous waste, poo has struggled since the dawn of time to receive the respect it deserves.

Even though everybody poos, societal norms dictate that issues pertaining to poo be kept private. The act of pooing is too often hastily and covertly performed. Rather than embracing its potential for catharsis, the world has rendered the act of pooing to be an undesirable inevitability of everyday life. Indeed, poo has long resided in society's outhouse.

Through discussion of poo's diversity of shapes, sizes, colors, and smells, we hope to elucidate the inner workings of the gastro-intestinal tract and to highlight the essential role poo plays in our physical and emotional well-being. Consider, for example, the feeling of unbridled elation that results from unleashing the perfect poo. Although difficult to achieve, this Poo-phoria lends a feeling of ecstasy, even invincibility, that some have likened to the perfect buzz. Athletes have learned to harness this power of poo and frequently employ the Pre-Game Poo as a safe and *legal* way to enhance on-field performance.

Like life, however, poo is not always a bed of roses. All of us have surely experienced the agonizing lack of fulfillment that can come from hard, pebble-like bowel movements or the anguish of incessant, torrential diarrhea.

In the process of helping the reader to understand the inner workings of his or her digestive tract, this book will unlock the many heretofore unsolved mysteries of human poo . . .

. . . why do the bathroom stalls at work always seem crowded after lunch?

. . . what causes poo to float?

. . . is it normal to go to the bathroom three times a day?

. . . what's the link between poo and toothbrushes?

. . . can normal poo really be green?

. . . what's the deal with corn, anyway?

While this book's primary aim is to liberate poo from its most undeserving position in the societal sewer, it also seeks to free those individuals who have until now been unable to share their love for poo with others. In addition, like any good book, we hope this treatise on poo will open up new worlds and offer new perspectives. So grab a seat (or squat) and get ready for the answers to the question "What's your poo telling you?"

Déjà Poo

Synonyms: *Veggie Burger, Leftovers, Corn-Backed Rattler, Sloppy Seconds*

"Haven't I seen that somewhere before?" Most notoriously involving corn, Déjà Poo is perhaps the most renowned and befuddling of all poos. A Déjà Poo is a bowel movement that has remarkably familiar portions of a recent meal embedded in it. This poo can include a potpourri of colors, often containing pieces of vegetables and other items that look as though they do not belong among the mass of poo in which they are entrenched. When producing this kind of turd, you may wonder whether you chewed sufficiently or whether your body extracted any of the nutrients from the food you just ate. You may also wonder how your body can process heavy meats and pastas but not an innocuous kernel of corn.

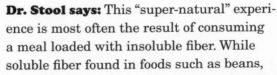

Dr. Stool says: This "super-natural" experience is most often the result of consuming a meal loaded with insoluble fiber. While soluble fiber found in foods such as beans, nuts, and carrots forms a gel-like substance when

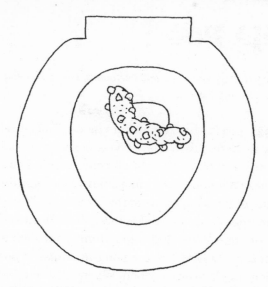

mixed with stomach secretions, the insoluble fiber contained in oat bran (and yes, corn on the cob) passes through the GI tract largely unchanged. Humans lack the necessary enzymes to digest certain components of plant cell walls. The presence of these indigestible remnants embedded in your feces is what gives rise to the sensation of Déjà Poo. Dr. Stool says consumption of high-fiber foods like corn and celery can soften the stool, thus yielding just as much enjoyment on the way out as on the way in.

ILLEGAL POO

In 1973, a young man was admitted to a Toronto hospital with symptoms of an intestinal blockage. An initial abdominal X-ray revealed a most unexpected diagnosis: intestinal obstruction from dozens of hashish-packed condoms. This case introduced the medical establishment to the illegal practice of "body packing." By employing people to ingest sometimes upward of a hundred cocaine- or heroin-filled latex balloons, drug traffickers utilize the intestinal tract to smuggle illicit substances past border security.

Body packers, it appears, have taken their own course in gastrointestinal physiology and have learned to manipulate the digestive tract for their benefit. These criminals use their knowledge of the gastro-colic reflex, a physiological condition in which the presence of food in the stomach triggers a rapid upsurge in intestinal contractions, and often go days without eating in order to avoid premature expulsion of their valuable contraband. To further shut down gastrointestinal motility, smugglers use medicines such as loperamide (Imodium), which are typically prescribed for patients plagued with severe diarrhea.

While bowel obstruction occurs on occasion, the most feared complication of body packing is balloon rupture. Balloon rupture results in a rapid release of lethal doses of cocaine or heroin into the GI tract. This catastrophic complication has been known to result in shock and, in severe cases, death. Once smugglers are apprehended, these packets are easily detected with an abdominal X-ray. "Treatment" is with laxatives (and close bathroom supervision!) to expedite the natural passage of these illicit goods.

Nuggets

The amount of stool expelled per day varies from country to country. For instance, South Asians unload nearly three times as much poo as their British counterparts. This difference is largely due to the higher fiber content in the average Indian diet.

Monster Poo

Synonyms: *Lincoln Log, The Crowd-Pleaser, Double Deuce, The Five-Minute Diet*

You may wonder, "How did something that large come out of me?" While sitting on the toilet and vigorously straining to discharge a poo of this size, you feel like the turd took a wrong turn in your intestines and is attempting to come out sideways. You may feel the swelling of veins in your forehead and the beading of perspiration as you toil to force this mass of poo out of your system. Despite the strain, this internal bodily struggle will continue until the last of the turd exits. After discharging this Double Deuce, it is not uncommon to feel as though you just lost five pounds. For a quick second, you may even consider summoning your friends to witness firsthand the greatness of your feat.

Despite the fact that these poos are not always the easiest to discharge, there is a great feeling of accomplishment and pride associated with the deposit of a Monster Poo. In addition to its massive girth, Monster Poo's most characteristic feature is its tendency to extend beyond the water surface. You may even fear flushing it without first using the toilet brush to break it up into smaller pieces. Despite the separation anxiety that may result, we recommend promptly flushing

continued

the toilet—after you have had a chance to bask in the glory of your poo.

 Dr. Stool says: Although studies have not correlated the degree of straining with the size of the bowel movement, several factors play a role in creating a glacier-size turd. The "bulk" of the stool is directly related to the amount of fiber and water you consume. Picture the engorged appearance of your favorite legume after soaking it overnight in a bowl of water! A similar reaction takes place in the gut, where soluble fiber and water combine to form a swollen mass of turd.

ANCIENT POO

The study of poo not only gives us valuable information about our current digestive health, but can yield valuable information about the behaviors of the animals that roamed the Earth millions of years ago. The study of coprolites, or fossilized poo, is widely used by paleontologists to better understand the dietary habits of dinosaurs. The largest dino poo ever excavated was found in Alberta, Canada, and measured 25 1/5 inches in length. Not impressed?  Keep in mind that the *T. rex* turd has undergone considerable shrinkage (65 million years' worth).

Poo-phoria

Synonyms: *Holy Crap, Mood Enhancer, The Tingler*

This poo can turn an atheist into a believer and is distinguished by the sense of euphoria and ecstasy that you feel throughout your body when this type of feces departs your system. The exhilaration from this defecation, large in volume but varying in form, is often accompanied by goose bumps and even a little light-headedness as the discharge of the toxins is completed. You feel energized, as if you just woke up from a great nap. To some it may feel like a religious experience, to others like an orgasm, and to a lucky handful it may feel like both. This is the type of poo that makes us all look forward to spending time on the toilet.

Dr. Stool says: This stool "high" is relatively safe, but can become an addiction for those who can willfully reproduce the sensation. The distention of the rectum that occurs with the passing of a large mass of stool causes the vagus nerve to fire. The net effect of this is a drop in your heart rate and blood pressure, which in turn decreases blood flow to the brain. When mild, the lightheadedness can lend a sense of sublime relaxation (the "high"). A more significant drop in brain perfusion can cause "defecation syncope," a dangerous syndrome that results in a transient loss of consciousness (the O.D., or Over-Doodie).

Nuggets

Ancient Egyptian tombs had special toilet chambers for the pharaohs to use on their way to the afterlife.

Dunce Cap

Synonyms: *Conehead, Tapered Wafer, Biggie Small*

As this type of bowel movement begins, you strain and feel like you are on the precipice of another Monster Poo (page 18). However, when the cork is popped and the poo begins to leave your body, it becomes exponentially easier from beginning to end as the bowel movement flows out. After completion, when you gaze at your conquest, you notice that the poo began with a thick base but then scaled down to a point. While you feel refreshed now that you have finished defecating, you wonder whether the initial pain and strain were necessary. You long for a more uniform poo, where the bulk is more evenly distributed.

Dr. Stool says: Remember when your mother said, "Don't try to be something you're not"? You had no idea this sage advice would apply to your defecating practices. The tapering appearance arises from one's attempt to craft an otherwise modest amount of stool into a long, robust log (as in kindergarten, when you tried to roll a long snake out of a small piece of clay). The narrow ending is a result of your continued straining and the pinching motion of your external anal sphincter (like squeezing the last bit of icing out of a pastry bag).

Plagued with one too many Coneheads? Try relaxing on the toilet. Resist that urge to contract your abdominal muscles in order to more quickly expel the log. Find a quiet, isolated stall where you won't feel pressured to quickly finish the deed. Still finding yourself tensing up at the wrong moment? May we recommend reading a good book about poo to help you "loosen up."

Doo You Know
The average weight of stool excreted a day is 450 grams (about a pound).

Performance-Enhancing Poo

Synonyms: *Anxiety Poo, Preparatory Poo, Running Runs, The Pre-Game Poo*

Sometimes intentional and other times triggered by nerves, the Pre-Game Poo is standard both for competitive athletes and for people with high-pressure presentations looming on the horizon. You never want to have to take a break in the middle of a key proposal or sale, and it would be unheard of to call a time-out for a mid-game bathroom break. With empty bowels, you can run faster and jump higher. Similarly, the absence of stool in your colon will make your presentation

crisper and diminish fears of an unscheduled pit stop or a loud gaseous emission. Unplanned Performance-Enhancing Poos often take on a more liquid consistency than their planned counterparts. Although these poos may not have the grandeur of some, their timing is critically important.

Dr. Stool says: The effect of stress on the GI tract is widely known. What has only recently been discovered, however, is that this stress-induced abdominal cramping and urge to defecate is caused not solely by the brain's messaging, but by the intestines' release of hormones and neurotransmitters. The "enteric nervous system" is a complex array of nerve fibers that is remarkably independent in its ability to regulate the digestive system. Columbia professor Dr. Michael Gershon definitively demonstrated our "second brain's" autonomy when he performed a classic experiment on a guinea pig colon. After surgically removing the colon from the guinea pig, he showed how a pellet placed at one end caused coordinated colonic contractions that quickly resulted in expulsion of the pellet from the other end. This confirms the suspicion that your GI tract has a mind of its own!

THE POWER OF POO

- In the Wild West, settlers burned dried buffalo chips to keep warm.

- In rural India, people pat cow manure into round disks and press them onto walls to dry. After the poo dries and falls off the walls, it is burned for heat. India burns approximately one-quarter of all the dung produced by the sacred cows.

- When you flush the toilet, your poo enters the sewage system and ends up at a wastewater treatment facility. There, it ferments into biogas, and biogas can be another source for power generation. Biogas typically refers to a gas produced by the anaerobic digestion or fermentation of organic matter, including manure, sewage sludge, municipal solid waste, or any other biodegradable feedstock, under anaerobic conditions. Biogas is composed primarily of methane and carbon dioxide. If biogas from a wastewater treatment facility were captured and used to power a fuel cell, each person's poo could produce approximately 2 watts of electricity per day.

• As we attempt to increase energy security and confront our addiction to oil, some have advocated the increased burning of human and animal dung for alternative energy sources. While the ideal poo is often described as soft and moist, it is the constipated, rock-hard stool that is most useful for energy production. Desiccated poo is more efficient due to its lower water content, thereby decreasing the energy needed to extract water prior to its combustion (the normal human stool is 90 percent water).

Floaters vs. Sinkers

Synonyms: *Aircraft Carrier vs. Submarine, The Buoy vs. The Anchor*

One of the most mystifying characteristics of poo is the tendency of some turds to float and others to sink to the bottom of the bowl. Whether big or small, brown or black, it is impossible to predict whether a poo will be a Floater or a Sinker until it hits the water and settles in. The obvious benefit of a Floater is that it won't leave racing stripes (see page 44) in the bowl. However, some stubborn Floaters have been known to resurface after multiple flushes, a distant cousin of the Déjà Poo (page 14).

Dr. Stool says: There are two components of stool that cause it to hover on the surface of the toilet water: gas and fat. Most commonly, Floaters are due to the fourth burrito or second helping of chili from the day before. When gas is the culprit, you may also notice your fart frequency increasing above normal levels. If the

Floaters last for a day or so, there is no reason to be alarmed.

Foul-smelling (I mean, really foul), greasy, floating stool is more worrisome. It usually indicates the presence of fat in the stool. This is never normal and often reflects an underlying problem in the GI tract, most commonly involving the pancreas or liver. The pancreas, liver, and gall bladder normally team up to help the body digest the fat we consume. When these organs become diseased, dietary fat passes through our GI tract largely undigested and results in the formation of floating, "oil-slick" stool.

Doo You Know

The most stubborn of Floaters seem to defy gravity and will not succumb to numerous flushing attempts. The way to eradicate these obstinate poos is to add additional water to the toilet tank in order to flush it down with more force.

BEANS, BEANS, THE MORE
YOU EAT . . .

Venezuelan researchers have bioengineered beans that cause less flatulence. By mixing beans with two species of bacteria, they found that rats had 88 percent less raffinose, a gas-forming compound. The question remains, do these beans taste good in a burrito? Skeptics predict the beans will take on a more tangy flavor akin to that of sauerkraut and sourdough bread, foods that employ a similar pre-fermentation process

Not crazy about tangy-tasting beans? Enjoy legumes the old-fashioned way by loading up on some alpha-D-galactosidase, the active ingredient in gas-reducing substances like Beano. This enzyme digests the otherwise indigestible polysaccharides high up in the digestive tract and thus prevents their passage into the colon, where voracious gas-forming bacteria reside.

FOODS THAT CAUSE GAS

- Beans
- Vegetables, such as broccoli, cabbage, brussels sprouts, onions, artichokes, and asparagus
- Fruits, such as pears, apples, and peaches
- Whole grains
- Soft drinks
- Milk
- Sorbitol (used as a sugar substitute in diet foods)

HIGH-FIBER FOODS (FOODS WITH HIGHEST FIBER CONTENT)

- Whole grains
- Vegetables (peas, artichokes, brussels sprouts, turnips)
- Fruits (pears, figs, blueberries)
- Legumes (lentils, black beans)
- Nuts (almonds, pistachios)

Braille Poo

Synonyms: *Baby Ruth, Porcupine, Rocky Road*

Despite the fact that all poo follows the same route through the GI tract before coming to rest in the toilet bowl, individual bowel movements can have markedly different textures. While some bowel movements are smooth and silky, others take on a more angular and bumpy appearance. Braille Poo can be identified by its rough and uneven texture. The passing of these uneven poos makes you wonder what causes this type of potholed feces and why they all can't achieve the honeyed smoothness of previous poos. However, it is important to accept that just as some roads are well paved while others are gravel or cobblestone, poo's texture can similarly be quite varied.

Dr. Stool says: This amalgam of poo appears to be due to a "catch-up" phenomenon. The slowing of colonic transit (i.e., constipation) allows digestive debris from several meals to form a single, variegated bolus of stool. In other words, the ham-and-cheese sandwich you had for lunch "runs into" the scrambled eggs you had for breakfast, the steak you had for dinner the night before, etc. Identifying remnants of prior meals can be both challenging and enjoyable. Unlike Déjà Poo (page 14), where the food item is identified largely unchanged in the turd, Braille Poo requires careful scrutiny of the stool's color, texture, and occasionally odor in order to correctly identify the individual components.

Nuggets

Studies of healthy subjects have revealed a wide variation in stool frequency. The current accepted range for "normal" is from three bowel movements per day to three bowel movements per week.

The Chinese Star

Synonyms: *The Dorito, Iceberg, Glass Shard, Mystery Poo*

This poo's defining characteristic is the excruciatingly painful sensation of feeling as if your rectum is being torn apart from the inside as the turd exits your body. This searing agony is commonly the result of passing a particularly hard, angular bowel movement. At times, this stool's appearance can be a source of bewilderment. As we hold back the flow of tears, our awareness quickly shifts to the identification of the offending particle. The mounting rage, however, is diffused when we gaze into the waters only to see a small, seemingly innocuous turd resting peacefully on the bottom of the toilet bowl.

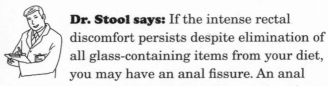

Dr. Stool says: If the intense rectal discomfort persists despite elimination of all glass-containing items from your diet, you may have an anal fissure. An anal fissure is a tear in the lining of the anal sphincter, usually occurring after passing a particularly hard stool. This break in the lining causes spasm of the internal anal sphincter (similar to any other muscle cramp) and can make having a bowel movement feel as if you are passing razor blades. Treatment consists of topical anesthetics, stool-softening agents, and sitz baths.

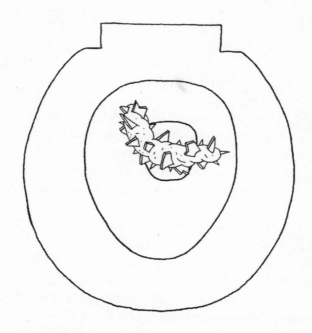

Rambo Poo

Synonyms: *Uh-Oh, Chocolate Sundae with Strawberry Sauce, The Neapolitan Poo*

On rare instances, you may look down at your droppings and see traces of blood. Despite the tone of this book (and the title of this poo), this is no laughing matter and could represent several different serious problems that you should consult a physician about.

 Dr. Stool says: Thankfully, there are many benign causes of blood in the toilet bowl, such as hemorrhoids, diverticulosis, and arteriovenous malformations (abnormal blood vessels that have a tendency to bleed). Before overreacting, keep in mind what happens when you put a few drops of food coloring into a bucket of water. Similarly, a few small drops of blood will convert your toilet into a large, unwelcome bowl of fruit punch.

Often overlooked, vigorous overwiping, which causes a little blood to appear on the ol' brown starfish, could also be the cause of the bloody surprise. In this case, consider yoga, exercise, or a new hobby for alternative stress relief. A conversion to a softer toilet paper would also be prudent.

However, the most feared cause of blood in the stool is colon cancer. Due to the seriousness of this illness, any new sighting of reddish stool or blood-tinged toilet water should always be followed by a visit to your doctor. In most cases of gastrointestinal bleeding, a colonoscopy is performed to visualize the interior of the GI tract and identify the source of bleeding.

Nuggets

One of the most distressing complications of inflammatory bowel disease is the formation of fistulae, which are abnormal connections between the diseased intestine and surrounding abdominal organs. These atypical conduits are often discovered when stool is seen exiting the body from such unusual locations as the abdominal wall. If a connection forms between the intestines and the bladder, a patient may actually complain of "passing stool" while he urinates! Historically, fistula treatment required surgery, but use of powerful anti-inflammatory medications can now lead to successful closure of these abnormal connections.

Number Three

Synonyms: *Butt Piss, Liquid Poo, The Runs, Oil Spill, Hershey Squirts, Montezuma's Revenge, Chocolate Thunder, Diarrhea, Operation Marination, Operation Evacuation, Releasing the Hounds, The Nile, Poo Stew, Chocolate Slurpee, Gravy Poo, Birds Flying South for the Winter, Rectum Rapids, It's Raining Poo, Deuce Juice, Turd Tea*

Although you know that you need to sit down for this rear deposit, Number Threes come in a liquid form and have little to no texture. When passing one, you feel as if you are urinating from the wrong side. A Number Three is often a violent discharge, sometimes with very little warning, and may often be accompanied by tremendous gaseous emissions. As you feel its sudden onset, your sense of relief that you made it to the toilet in time is quickly replaced by the ill feeling associated with the release of a Number Three. The explosiveness is so severe that it often results in brown splatter hitting the underside of the toilet seat. At times, the splatter is so great that you have to wipe remnants off your butt cheeks when you are finished. Number Threes are not pleasant.

continued

Dr. Stool says: To understand the Number Three, one must understand the factors that are responsible for producing the prototypical semisolid bolus. The stool's desired consistency is formed by a careful balance of fluid secretion/absorption and intestinal transit time. Perturbations in this system can result in the extremes of the stooling experience: from bowel-breaking constipation to torrential watery diarrhea.

The Number Three has two main causes: GI tract infections and maldigestion. Inadvertent consumption of bacteria, viruses, or toxins from undercooked meat or week-old potato salad causes the small bowel to secrete large volumes of fluid into the GI tract. This deluge of fluid, coupled with brisk intestinal transit (picture the torrent of Class 5 rapids), results in the delivery of large amounts of liquid to the rectum. Cholera infection is the most severe example of this physiology. The diarrhea produced by this disease is classically referred to as having the consistency of "rice water" and leads rapidly to life-threatening dehydration.

Impaired digestion is the other possible cause of the Number Three. One should consider this diagnosis when the explosiveness of the bowel movement is particularly violent. In lactose-intolerant individuals, ingestion of dairy products results in the production of copious amounts of gas and liquid stool. If severe enough, the expulsion of these "contents under pressure" can cause your significant other to run for cover.

LONG BOMB

On thankfully rare occasions, stool is expelled in an uncontrollable and violent manner. This explosion of gas and liquid almost always occurs in the setting of a gastrointestinal infection. However, our ability as a species to volitionally expel our poo even a few inches is severely limited (go ahead, try). Contrast our shortcomings to the defecating habits of the skipper caterpillar, which can propel its stool over five feet in the air! Thought to be a defense mechanism against predators that track caterpillar excrement, this remarkable feat would be the equivalent of the average human being launching his or her stool over two hundred feet!

The Streak

Synonyms: *Skidmark, Hershey Highway, Racing Stripe, Lining the Pavement*

A phrase more commonly reserved for Joe DiMaggio's seemingly unbreakable fifty-six-game hitting streak in 1941, The Streak also has a well-established place in the world of poo. The Streak is a relic of a prior poo usually appearing as a thin brown stain down the center of the toilet bowl. Some streaks maintain their legacy and remain visible for multiple flushes after their original introduction to the toilet. The appearance of a racing stripe at the bottom of the bowl is a most unwelcome sight for all would-be poopers, especially guests at a friend's dinner party. While one's first notion is to curse the streak's creator, it must be acknowledged that in a majority of cases the rightful owner of this chocolate drizzle is oblivious to its existence. This ignorance is attributable to the fact that The Streak appears only after completion of the flush. To ensure you don't leave a poo trail that leads to you, always give the post-flush glance to make sure you don't need an encore flush.

Dr. Stool says: While this is no streak to be proud of, it is rarely a cause for concern. The appearance of The Streak is highly unpredictable, and there is no evidence to suggest that specific foods are responsible for lending this stool its sticky nature. One potentially worrisome scenario associated with thick, sticky stools is upper gastrointestinal bleeding. In this case, blood originating from "high up" in the GI tract (i.e., the stomach) is transformed during its passage through the intestines into a thick, tarry stool that is usually jet black in color and extremely foul smelling. A dramatic change in the color of stool (to either black or red) can often be the first indication of serious gastrointestinal bleeding.

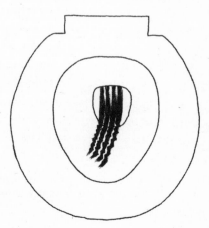

Sneak Attack

Synonyms: *Ambush Poo, Chocolate Surprise, Deuce Is Loose, Shart*

Regardless of our readiness to "come clean," we have all gambled and lost in this sinister game of shooting craps. We look for a lucky seven, but alas roll snake eyes. It usually starts with the uncomfortable sensations of intestinal rumbling and gaseous bloating. Thinking that a quick, surreptitious release of gas will usher in much needed relief, you prepare for an airy evacuation. But occasionally the anticipated fart contains more than just gas and is accompanied by a liquid smear of poo. In addition to staining your underwear, the smelly remnants of this Sneak Attack will follow you around until you perform the necessary cleaning . . . usually a hasty laundering in the bathroom sink. When faced with a Sneak Attack, we recommend taking care of the cleanup immediately. Often this may require throwing away your underwear and going commando for the rest of the day. A refreshing shower should eliminate all remaining traces of this unwelcome surprise—both physically and emotionally.

Dr. Stool says: This fecal surprise is due to the presence of liquid stool in the rectum, the antechamber where stool is stored before expulsion. Distension of the rectum (by stool or air) causes the urge to empty the rectum's contents. Normally, solid stool is easily kept inside the vault, but in the setting of significant, watery diarrhea, stool can inadvertently escape when the anal sphincter opens to release gas.

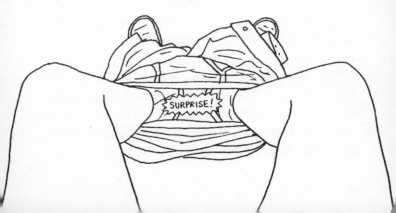

Soft Serve

Synonyms: *Jabba the Poo, Play Doo, Cow Pattie, Septic Seepage*

More dense than diarrhea but softer than a normal poo, this solid yet amorphous turd comes out in one smooth, steady flowing motion. Its easy exit may make you feel like the stool will take a liquid form, but you are pleasantly surprised to see its more cohesive consistency when you are done. While still far from a cylindrical shape, these poos look a lot like cow patties. If you deposited this poo directly into a bowl, it would be easy to mistake for a dish of soft-serve ice cream from Dairy Queen on a hot summer day (although the odor would help make the distinction quite clear). This form of poo sometimes comes as a precursor to, or a last stage of, some sort of intestinal disturbance.

Dr. Stool says: Stool's liquid consistency can be intermittent, often varying from one bowel movement to the next. When short-lived, the development of mildly loose stools associated with abdominal cramping is usually due to ingestion of poorly absorbed foodstuffs. While substances such as fructose (in juices and sodas) and sorbitol (in sugar-free gum) are becoming increasingly recognized, the most common cause of the Soft Serve is lactose intolerance.

Lactose intolerance—the inability to digest the main sugar found in milk—is a remarkably common condition worldwide, especially within certain ethnic groups. Asian and African American populations have rates of lactose intolerance that approach 80 percent. Lactase, the enzyme responsible for breaking down lactose, is found exclusively in the small intestine and is affected by a variety of conditions. While most lactose-intolerant individuals are genetically deficient in lactase, conditions such as inflammatory bowel disease, which injure the small intestine, can also reduce levels of the lactase enzyme. Lactose intolerant and craving that extra-thick milk shake? Try taking supplemental lactase

continued

enzyme pills to help process the load. Another way to enjoy your morning cereal if you are lactose-intolerant is to subsitute soy milk, which has the added benefit of adding protein to your diet.

If you know your Soft Serve is not being caused by lactose intolerance, you should ask your doctor if you have celiac sprue, a disease characterized by an intolerance to gluten-containing foods. Gluten is a component of grains such as wheat, rye, and barley, and ingestion by susceptible individuals causes an immune reaction that damages the small intestine. Crampy abdominal pain, watery diarrhea, and the eventual development of an iron deficiency (anemia) are common adult manifestations of this condition. Diagnosis can be made by blood tests and upper endoscopy. Treatment requires the elimination of all gluten from one's diet.

More often than not, this form of poo does not require specific treatment. An increase in dietary fiber will help to bulk up the stool and lend it a more traditional consistency.

POO IN THE
ANIMAL KINGDOM

• Rabbits can produce more than five hundred pellets of poo every day.

• Horses poo ten pounds' worth of dung, often without breaking stride.

• Geese poo, on average, once every twelve minutes.

• Bears don't poo at all when hibernating. Their bodies create an internal plug, made from feces and hair, that prevents them from pooing while sleeping.

D.A.D.S.

Synonyms: *Revenge of the Poo, Morning After, Poo of Shame, Bud Mud*

A D.A.D.S. is a day-after-drinking stool. After a long night of partying, you may awake the next day with a hangover and an unsettled stomach. Whether your personal hangover cure is a greasy meal, a milk shake, a Bloody Mary, or a family elixir, your body needs to purge itself of the toxins and recover from the indulgences of the previous evening. A D.A.D.S. often comes in a semisolid state, and sometimes is accompanied by stomach discomfort. The most notable trait of a D.A.D.S. is the tread mark left on the toilet bowl after you flush, as well as the distinctive bar-floor smell. The more you drank

the night before, the more D.A.D.S. you need to eliminate to start feeling better. Usually your second D.A.D.S. of the day signifies that your recovery is well under way.

Dr. Stool says: The runs you experience the morning after are due to ethanol's stimulant effect on your bowel's motility: It basically "revs" up the intestines so that the contents move through more quickly. This leaves less time for your colon to absorb water, and results in a profuse, watery stool. Occasionally, the large carbohydrate load in alcoholic beverages can overwhelm your digestive enzymes and indirectly cause diarrhea.

HANGOVERS

1. Darker spirits (tequila, brandy, wine) are more likely to cause hangovers than lighter ones (rum, gin, vodka).

2. Treatments for hangovers include rehydration, vitamin B_6, and possibly medicines that decrease prostaglandin production (like ibuprofen).

The Green Goblin

Synonym: *Seaweed Stool*

The Green Goblin, though thankfully rare, is an explosion of foul-smelling diarrhea that is characterized by its viridian hue. Although various foods can lend normal poo a greenish tint, this bowel movement's deep-set, blackish green appearance makes it seem as if you are viewing it through night-vision goggles. Also distinguishing this poo from more benign green poos is its liquid form and associated symptoms of fever and abdominal pain. More often than not, this poo transformation occurs following a course of antibiotics for a tooth abscess or sinus infection.

 Dr. Stool says: This diarrheal illness is caused by the overgrowth of a specific bacterium in the colon called *Clostridium difficile.* The use of the antibiotics upsets the natural balance of "good" and "bad" bacteria in our intestines and allows the proliferation of this particularly harmful organism, which, in turn, results in inflammation of the colonic lining and causes profuse diarrhea, abdominal pain, and fever. Medical treatment is with a different type of antibiotic that specifically attacks *Clostridium difficile*.

Doo You Know

The consumption of yogurt can help with mild forms of diarrhea caused by antibiotics. Yogurt contains active bacterial cultures that help to repopulate the GI tract with colon-friendly organisms that may have been wiped out by high-powered antibiotics. The importance of these "good" bacteria is being increasingly recognized and has resulted in the creation of the "probiotic" movement. Supporters believe that consuming certain species of "good" bacteria can help prevent and treat various gastrointestinal ailments. Some have even gone so far as to claim benefits with regards to preventing cancer, treating hypertension, and lowering cholesterol.

STOOL TRANSPLANT

We have all heard of patients whose lives are saved by receiving a new heart, kidney, or liver. One of the most recent advancements in transplantation involves the transferring of stool from one person's colon to another! This seemingly barbaric practice has been shown to help patients recover from a form of colitis caused by the bacterium *Clostridium difficile*. After the collection and processing of the donated stool, the feces are placed into the patient's small intestine via an endoscopic tube. Typically used as a last resort, this treatment seeks to correct the colon's bacterial imbalance by repopulating the gut with billions of healthful bacteria from a healthy volunteer. Whereas the waiting list for organs can grow quite long, the future of stool transplantation appears promising, owing to the short list of willing recipients and the potentially endless supply of donors.

The Snake

Synonyms: *Curly Fry, The Long Thin Line, Fettuccine Feces*

The Snake is a thin and windy defecation that can contort itself into a variety of different shapes and sizes. Some Snakes wrap around the bottom of the toilet bowl clockwise, and others go counterclockwise. Some Snakes twist themselves into the

continued

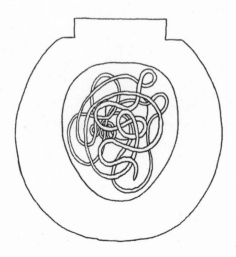

shape of a pretzel, while others zig-zag across the bowl. Regardless of the final form, Snakes seem to go on forever as they leave your rectum. In the end, however, Snakes never leave you with the same feeling of accomplishment as do poos of a wider diameter.

 Dr. Stool says: Excessive straining usually forms this long, thin stool. The act of bearing down causes contraction of the external anal sphincter (the "valve" that opens in order to allow feces to exit the rectum). Contraction of this muscle narrows the aperture through which the stool bolus passes, thus creating your garter snake–morphed turd. While everyone will occasionally produce these slender stools, progressive narrowing in stool caliber over months can indicate the presence of a rectal cancer. These "pencil-thin" stools are formed as the rectal tumor's growth gradually narrows the colonic cavity.

SPAGHETTI "POO"

When is a poo not really a poo? The passage of this noodle-like strand may at first seem to be a particularly slender thread of stool. Closer inspection, however, will reveal that this poo imitator is, in fact, a parasite known as *Ascaris lumbricoides*. These worms, somewhat reminiscent of angel hair pasta, can grow to be over a foot long. They reside quietly for years in the small intestine and may only come to attention during their dramatic exit. Rarely, these worms can cause nutritional deficiency by competing with your GI tract for valuable nutrients. Think you have a worm? You're probably not alone; research has shown that one-quarter of the world's population is infected with this roundworm.

Pebble Poo

Synonyms: *Rabbit Poo, Kibbles 'n' Bits, Splashers, Butt Hail, Blueberries, Buckshot, Meteor Shower*

You may sit down at the toilet with aspirations for a large, enjoyable poo, only to have Pebble Poos leave you unsatisfied and unfulfilled. Despite your vigorous straining and the sensation of poo exiting your rectum, when you stand up to look there are only a handful of pebbles resting mockingly on the toilet bowl floor. Adding insult to injury are the unwelcome splashes that hit your buttocks as the mini poo pellets hit the water.

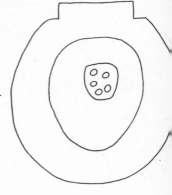

Dr. Stool says: Pebble Poo reflects a lack of stool cohesion. How does the GI tract produce a well-congealed, singular bolus of soft stool? It uses glue, of course. This "glue" is actually a fatty-acid gel that is formed when ingested fiber is fermented by bacteria residing in the colon. This sticky substance, not unlike the gooey marshmallow mixture in Rice Krispies treats, keeps poo from breaking apart and drying out. This magical gel also lubricates the inside of the colon, allowing the stool bolus to pass friction-free through the GI tract. A lack of dietary fiber results in small, hard, disjointed poos that can give rise to the most un-Zen-like of stooling experiences.

Doo You Know

Humans lack the enzymes necessary to digest cellulose, the main constituent in high-fiber foods. Cows, too, lack these necessary enzymes, but are able to digest the cellulose found in plant cell walls by utilizing enzymes produced by bacteria residing in their intestines.

Log Jam

Synonyms: *Ghost Poo, Can't Get the Train Out of the Tunnel, Colon Congestion, Corked, F.O.S., Stuck Up, Crying Wolf, False Alarm*

Even worse than Pebble Poo (page 60) is no poo at all. Despite stomach pains, rancid gas, and feeling a turd on deck, no matter how hard you push, nothing comes out. After ten to fifteen minutes in the bathroom, your friends, spouse, or roommate may start to worry about you, but you may not be ready to give up yet. However, when you ultimately decide that it was a false call, the emptiness of the toilet bowl is a cruel reminder of your inability to perform.

 Dr. Stool says: This is the most feared complication of constipation. A lack of dietary fiber and water can result in a stool bolus so hard and so firm that it is unable to pass through the anal sphincter. Whereas normal stool is able to smoothly and effortlessly exit the rectum, a desiccated boulder-like bolus often cannot escape its confinement without assistance. Treatment entails the administration of enemas and, in severe cases, manual disimpaction. Want to avoid this unpleasant, intrusive manipulation? Dr. Stool recommends that your diet contain an ample amount of fiber and water.

POOLESS JOE JACKSON

In the early 1900s, a teenage boy suffered for many years from abdominal distension and bloating. His family and physicians noted that he rarely had bowel movements and that his abdomen ballooned in size, but the underlying etiology of his affliction remained a mystery until after his premature death from intestinal perforation. An autopsy revealed a dilated, cavernous colon, chock-full of foul-smelling stool. This young man likely suffered from what is now known as Hirschsprung's disease, a congenital disease in which there is an absence of the nerve cells that are responsible for propelling stool through the colon. This "intestinal paralysis" results in an inability to defecate and causes progressive stretching of the intestines, eventually (if untreated) leading to intestinal rupture. This disease is the most extreme manifestation of the Log Jam and is widely regarded as the most severe form of constipation.

Gift Poo

Synonyms: *Pollyanna Poo, Phantom Poo, Surprise Party, Shock and Awe, Flushless Folly, River Pickle*

Gift Poos are turds that people leave behind in toilets without flushing. They come in all shapes and sizes and are most prevalent in public restrooms and fraternity houses. These gifts are sometimes left as trophies to anonymously show off accomplishments, or as pranks, or occasionally as absent-minded accidents (often resulting from multitaskers trying to talk on their cell phone and wanting to avoid the flush that gives them away). The origins of these poos may remain a mystery, but they can linger anywhere from minutes to days, depending on when the gift is first seen or smelled.

 Dr. Stool says: Stool can remain for days, even weeks, submerged in the friendly confines of a toilet bowl. Whereas some turds retain their cohesion and luster for extended periods of time, the usual Gift Poo will gradually fragment and liquefy.

Ring of Fire

Synonyms: *Acid Poo, Hooters Souvenir, Curry in a Hurry, Fire in the Hole, Tabasco Turd, Feeling the Burn*

Sometimes, you sit down to do your business and a burning sensation rips through your anus. As every millimeter of poo passes through you, the burning only gets more excruciating. It may feel as though someone is funneling hydrochloric acid through your sphincter, and you may scream out, "Why?!?!?" As you pray for the poo to end and the burning to dissipate, you think back on what you have done to deserve this agony.

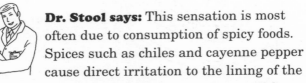 **Dr. Stool says:** This sensation is most often due to consumption of spicy foods. Spices such as chiles and cayenne pepper cause direct irritation to the lining of the gastrointestinal tract. The exquisite pain felt upon defecating should come as no surprise because a similar burning sensation was surely experienced in the mouth during consumption of the spicy food. The similarity in sensation can be attributed

to the fact that the inner layer of the mouth and the anus are lined by the same type of cell. These "squamous" cells, unlike the "columnar" cells lining the majority of the gastrointestinal tract, are able to discriminate among multiple stimuli, none more dramatic than its preception of five-alarm chili.

Camouflage Poo

Synonyms: *Dalmatian Dookie, Chocolate Chip Cookie Doo, Black and Tan, Olive Loaf*

A reference to a multitoned poo (varying shades of black, brown, and green), Camouflage Poo looks like a mosaic of diverse excrement from different sources and from assorted meals. While it is all one unit of poo, it resembles a conglomerate rock, with many pieces of poo forced together by the impact of time and pressure. Due to their camouflage coloring, such poos have historically been difficult to identify in the wilderness. Thankfully, the present-day practice of using toilets affords us a pristine white backdrop against which we can carefully examine these poos. While the size of this type of turd varies, the texture is usually bumpy and the appearance unmistakable.

Dr. Stool says: Stool can come in many different colors. Our stool's usual brown color is due to the presence of a compound called stercobilin, which is formed when the bacteria in our colon digest bile. Most daily variation in stool color is due to the dietary intake of various foods and medications. However, changes in stool color that persist for longer periods of time can be a sign of an underlying gastrointestinal disorder.

The following chart can help explain the variations in poo hue.

Black	Iron pills (or foods high in iron), bismuth compounds (i.e., Pepto-Bismol), blood (from higher up in digestive tract)
Red	Blood (from lower down in digestive tract), beets
White/Gray	Bile duct blockage, liver disease
Green	Gastrointestinal infection, spinach
Yellow	Fat in stool (pancreatic disease)

Hanging Chad

Synonyms: *Grundle Weeds, Cling-Ons, Butt Bark, The Lone Ranger, Turtle Head, Crap Crumbs*

It is critical when wiping up after a poo to make sure the job is complete. Hanging Chads are the stubborn pieces of turd that cling to the anal hairs and often refuse to let go. Larger than the traditional dingleberry, an unnoticed Hanging Chad can provide an unwelcome surprise when you remove your underwear or take a shower. While some find these surprises humorous, they can be disastrous if your lover is the one who discovers these leftovers. When such a calamity occurs, not even the U.S. Supreme Court can step in to save you. In order to dislodge the Lone Ranger, one may need to rock back and forth or utilize a bouncing motion at the end of the bowel movement. The last recourse, should these poo calisthenics fail, is to find a healthy piece of toilet paper (preferably double-ply) and utilize the unappealing, yet surprisingly effective, "pinch" maneuver. Tempted to obliterate the hanging chad by wiping more vigorously? Remember the old adage: "Fear the smear."

Dr. Stool says: These poo remnants are often a result of a hasty cleanup. They can be found still clinging to the anal region, either still attached to the anal sphincter or latching on like a little commando to the surrounding skin or hair. A cursory wipe will not do, especially when the poo's consistency is exceptionally viscous (picture dark maple syrup drippings adhering to tree bark). While the rocking maneuver and pinching technique are favored strategies for dealing with Hanging Chads, if an additional wipe is warranted we recommend the wiping be performed in a front-to-back fashion in order to generate the greatest degree of sheer force and to avoid contamination of the genital area.

Nuggets

In certain professions, constipation is an occupational hazard. Most common among truck drivers and those in the armed forces, the inability to have regular bowel movements is the result of years of having to "hold it in." The retention of stool leads to gradual stretching of the rectum and disrupts the normal reflex that triggers the urge to defecate.

Rotten Poo

Synonyms: *Napalm, Rancid Poo, Aftershock Poo, Agent Orange*

This poo can vary in shape and size, but its distinguishing feature is its atrocious and unbearable odor. As this poo is under way, the stench will overwhelm you. Even with a quick-response courtesy flush, survival instincts force you to speed up the defecating process in order to exit the bathroom as quickly as humanly possible. Lord help the innocent bystanders if you are in a public restroom, because this odor will linger and may promptly cause you and others to experience severe gagging and nausea. Worse than a rotten egg, worse than Limburger cheese, this poo smells as if a dead animal has been decomposing in your intestines and is making its exit at its most noxious moment. A Rotten Poo's odor is so powerful that anyone entering the vicinity within the next several hours is affected. There really is no way to prepare for a poo like this. However, when it happens, a quick termination of the stooling session is a must.

continued

Dr. Stool says: The compounds that lend poo (and farts) their odors are produced by the bacteria residing in our colon. These bacteria react with our ingested food to form smelly sulfur-containing compounds such as hydrogen sulfide and mercaptans. Occasionally, foul-smelling stools can be a sign of disease. Difficulties with digesting and absorbing food, as occurs in cystic fibrosis or chronic pancreatitis, can result in floating, greasy, and foul-smelling stool (see "Floaters vs. Sinkers," page 30). Intestinal infections, particularly with the parasite *Giardia lamblia*, can also cause diarrhea with an especially abhorrent odor. This infection is usually contracted after taking a dip in a freshwater lake or pond. Ingestion of even a small amount of contaminated water can be followed by several days of rancid diarrhea.

While persistent foul-smelling stool can be a sign of underlying disease, the occasional rotten-smelling poo should not be a cause for health concern. Your reputation at work, however, is a different story. If you deposit a Rotten Poo at work, Dr. Stool highly recommends leaving the stall of stench as quickly and stealthily as possible and taking a long walk outside while praying mightily that the smell hasn't permanently embedded itself in your clothes.

ENEMAS

The act of instilling liquids (usually water) into the rectum has been around for centuries. Historically known as "clysters," enemas were the preferred treatment of the bourgeoisie for a wide variety of gastrointestinal ailments. The medical history books are filled with examples of unusual uses and types of enemas. In fact, the expression "to blow smoke up her ass" comes from the practice of imparting tobacco smoke into the rectum of a fainting woman in attempts to revive her. Lest you  think that these practices were solely found in the eighteenth century, enemas consisting of coffee, alcohol, and even milk and honey are widely touted today by certain homeopaths as having beneficial effects on colonic health.

The Clean Sweep

Synonyms: *Wipeless Poo, The Perfect Wipe, Mr. Clean*
Antonyms: *The Wet Poo, Swamp Ass, Mudslide*

On rare and special occasions, you engage in
the entire stooling process from engagement to
deployment and note, in the cleanup phase, that
amazingly there is no poo residue on the toilet
paper! Despite coming up clean on the first wipe,
some skeptical souls wipe one more time just to
make sure there isn't a poo illusion at play. Some
experts consider the "wipeless" poo to be the
pinnacle of poo performance. You may depart the
restroom feeling extra clean after this type of poo.

This is in direct contrast to other times when
you use half the roll of toilet paper and feel as if you
haven't made any progress. What's worse is that
those moist, multi-wipe poos seem to occur at the
most inopportune times—e.g., in a crowded public
restroom where you only have a few inches of cheap,
single-ply, essentially transparent toilet paper.
In these instances, wiping can be so unsuccessful
that you end up putting toilet paper between your
butt cheeks to avoid painting your underwear with

skid marks. These situations, juxtaposed to Clean Sweeps, remind us that although there is little discernible difference during the exit, the cleanup can have dramatic variation.

Dr. Stool says: In your haste to triumphantly rush from the stall and high-five your co-workers to celebrate this most momentous achievement, do not forget to wash your hands! Stool contains between 150 and 500 different types of bacteria in a concentration of 10^{12} bacteria per gram! Even in the rare instance of the Wipeless Poo, there are sure to be a couple billion microscopic bacteria on the toilet paper (not to mention the mélange of microbes on the flush handle, the bathroom door, etc.). Some stooling conservatives have advocated for a change in nomenclature, arguing that "Clean Sweep" lends a false sense of hygienic security.

POO-THBRUSH?

Scientists have discovered the presence of *E. coli*, a bacterium commonly found in poo, during random testing of household toothbrushes! While your initial reaction may be to question how exactly other people are using their toothbrushes, it seems that

contamination occurs when airborne bacteria (launched by a toilet flush) land on the nearby dental-cleaning apparatus. This research has led to the recommendation by national dental agencies to store toothbrushes at least six feet away from toilets. Dr. Stool, although admittedly not a dentist, feels that closing your toilet lid prior to flushing may also be a good idea.

Postpartum Poo

Synonym: *Bonus Baby*

While many would-be mothers are prepared for the pain of childbirth, few are ready for what could end up being an even more painful delivery—the passing of the first Postpartum Poo. Typically occurring between one and three days after a vaginal delivery (sometimes even longer after a C-section), this bowel movement is a combination of the worst your GI tract has to offer. Some mathematically-inclined mothers have described this experience with the equation: Postpartum Poo = (Logjam + Ring of Fire)^2.

Dr. Stool says: Several factors contribute to the pain associated with a woman's first bowel movement after childbirth. First, the lengthy labor process fatigues and stretches the abdominal muscles, thereby making it difficult to generate sufficient expulsive force. Second, the trauma of a baby passing through the vaginal canal puts stress on all nearby organs including the colon, frequently "stunning" it

continued

into silence for a couple of hours to a few days. This "stunning" is even more pronounced when the bowel is manipulated during a C-section. Third, women frequently emerge from childbirth extremely dehydrated due to blood loss and the fact that they have been unable to eat or drink for many hours. This creates a hard, desiccated bolus of stool that makes passage more difficult. Fourth, by the end of pregnancy, nearly all women have engorged hemorrhoids. Irritation of these hemorrhoids can make defecation that much more painful. Finally, the presence of an episiotomy or vaginal tear during childbirth can create apprehension toward doing something as simple as sitting, let alone forcing out a rigid bolus of stool.

While the physiologic reality of the postpartum period cannot be changed, several steps may help to make the first few Postpartum Poos more tolerable. Increase water intake to 6 to 8 glasses a day, increase fiber intake, and take frequent walks to help soften the stool and kick-start your GI tract's engine. Gentle laxatives and enemas are also frequently needed in the early postpartum period. The most important thing to do

is to go early and go often. Ignoring the urge to poo
only makes the bolus harder and drier, making
its passage that much more unpleasant.

Doo You Know
A recent study showed that, while 95 percent of men
and women surveyed say they wash their hands
after using a public restroom, only 67 percent of
people actually do.

PEDIATRIC POO

Pediatric poos are unique in their appearance, texture, and aroma and are best thought of in terms of their likeness to various condiments and spreads.

• **Meconium** (Marmite): This is the dark and sticky stool produced in the first 24 to 48 hours after birth. It is formed during the fetus's nine months in utero and is remarkably odorless (a fetus's intestines are sterile and have yet to become overgrown with bacteria). Meconium shares its green-black color and pasty texture with Marmite, the pungent yeast-based spread of the Brits, and Vegemite, beloved by the Aussies, but thankfully lacks their overpowering aroma.

• **Breast-fed Poo** (Grey Poupon): The decision of whether to breast-feed or bottle-feed your child can be a difficult one. One important, yet often overlooked, aspect of the debate concerns the issue of poo. Put simply, the poo of a breast-fed baby can be a thing of beauty. Classically described as yellow and "seedy" in consistency, this poo is adored by parents for its sweet aroma. Given the similarities, this poo is often mistaken for a fine Dijon mustard.

- **Intussusception** (Currant Jelly): Intussusception is a form of intestinal blockage that occurs in infants and involves one portion of the intestine telescoping into another. While abdominal discomfort is the main symptom, the passage of a viscous, reddish black bowel movement can be an early clue to the diagnosis. The mixture of blood-tinged stool with mucus lends this poo its red currant jelly appearance.

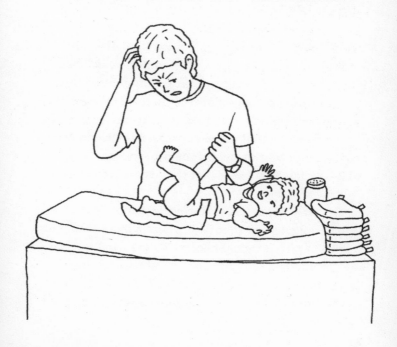

The Honeymoon's-Over Poo

Synonym: *The "I Do" Doo*

Courting and dating rituals may vary across cultures and time periods, but one constant is the anxiety involved in taking a dump while in the presence of your significant other. In the early stages of a relationship, many people come up with elaborate stories to avoid the issue, often suppressing the urge to poo for days at a time. Ultimately, as the relationship progresses, you begin to openly proclaim your desire to poo, eventually gaining the confidence to poo freely in that person's presence. Allowing your significant other to smell your poo without concern officially lets you know that the honeymoon is over.

 Dr. Stool says: Nature is full of examples suggesting that defecation is more than just a physiological necessity. One need look no further than at a cat hastily concealing its feces, a dog doing the reverse leg kick to separate himself from his deed, or a young child escaping to a

quiet corner of the room to appreciate the extremely
personal nature of this deed. Given the intimacy of
this process, it comes as no surprise that there is
an air of vulnerability surrounding this act. This
sentiment is embodied in the well-known saying,
"He was caught with his pants down." Allowing
oneself to "be caught" by another while performing
this most private of duties truly signifies the
development of an unwavering trust. Others would
say it's just weird.

The Ritual Poo

Synonyms: *Rite of Passage, Palm Poo, Calendar Crap*

This poo occurs at the same time each day. Due to the clockwork nature of this poo, you can prepare by having a newspaper ready and your favorite bathroom location scoped out ahead of time. The regularity of these poos may provide comfort in an otherwise unpredictable world.

Dr. Stool says:

"Just as the sun will rise . . . " The early-morning ritual poo can be a great start to the day. Some experience this poo only after consuming their ritual morning coffee (caffeine works as a laxative by increasing the colon's contractions). For others, the poo trigger is fired after each meal. This "postprandial" poo is caused by the gastrocolic reflex, where distension of the stomach by meal contents causes a reflex stimulation of the intestines, moving stool into the rectum and giving us the urge to defecate. (Translation: Out with the old, in with the new.) Need proof of this biological truth? Check out the bathroom stalls at work about a half-hour after lunch.

Nuggets

What's Poo Made Of?

- *10 parts water*
- *1 part bacteria (dead and alive)*
- *1 part indigestible fiber*
- *1 part mixture of fat, protein, dead cells, mucus*

The Sit vs. The Squat

For many of us, the act of squatting to "do the deed" conjures up images of less-fortunate children living in societies that lack modern plumbing. For others, stooping to poo has a more nostalgic significance, serving as a reminder of those quick dashes into the bushes for a country dump while camping.

The act of squatting, while seemingly rudimentary, can be fraught with great danger. As the novice squatter begins his descent, he becomes increasingly preoccupied with maintaining his balance while simultaneously ensuring that the stool's trajectory will avoid his pants, socks, and shoes. Inexperienced squatters who are accustomed to the 90-degree angle formed while sitting on the toilet may attempt to re-create this formation during squatting. Unfortunately, this leaves a great distance between poo deployment and landing and dramatically increases the risk of inadvertent lower-extremity soiling. An analogy can be drawn from the world of skydiving, where it is commonly taught that the higher you are when deploying a

continued

parachute, the less predictable your landing site will be.

Bottom line? When forced to squat, low is the way to go.

Dr. Stool says: Squatting is actually a more effective way of expelling stool than sitting on a toilet seat. A quick review of the physiology of defecation will illustrate this. The rectum is the storage site for stool prior to evacuation. It normally has a tortuous and windy course (picture San Francisco's Lombard Street) that must undergo straightening in order for stool to make its way through the anal canal prior to expulsion from the body. The act of squatting changes the orientation of a group of muscles called the *levator ani*, which actually serves to stretch open the accordion-shaped rectum. This creates a "straight shot" for the poo to effortlessly make its way out of the body. Just as some naturalists have touted the benefits of breast-feeding and natural childbirth, there is a burgeoning movement that believes squatting can improve digestive health. Not to mention the fact that squatting, also known as the bombardier method, will give you quads of steel.

THE CRAPPER

Thomas Crapper, a mid-nineteenth-century British plumber, is widely credited with inventing the toilet (though this is not, in fact, true). His name is also thought to have given rise to poo's most sophisticated synonym: crap. Other more likely origins for "crap" include the Dutch word *krappe*, from *krappen*, which means "to pluck off," and the German *krape*, which means a particularly disgusting and inedible fish.

Poo historians debate the origins of the term "crap," but most agree that Sir John Harrington designed the first flush toilet in 1596, 250 years before Crapper. However, since buildings had no plumbing to bring in the water to make the toilets flush in the sixteenth century, the introduction of the flush toilet had to wait until the nineteenth century, when Crapper was falsely credited with introducing the modern flushing toilet.

Curtain Call

Synonyms: *Overtime, Groundhog Day, The Remix*

Sometimes you finish defecating, wipe, pull up your pants, flush the toilet, and suddenly feel a stomach grumble. Despite the fact that you thought you were done with your business, your GI tract is ostensibly ringing the bell for Round 2, and you need to get back in the ring. If you don't answer the call, things could get ugly, fast.

Dr. Stool says: Yet another instance in which the sequel turns out not to be as good as the original. This poo most often occurs as a result of a normal physiologic process termed the MMC, or migrating motor complex. Occurring at 90-minute intervals, the MMC is a massive sweeping motion of the colon that quickly propels stool downstream (picture a huge tidal wave crashing ashore). If one of these waves happens to "refill" the rectum after you thought you finished the deed, there's nothing to do but unleash the second edition. On the bright side, at least the toilet seat will be warm.

continued

However, the feeling of constantly needing to empty one's bowels, known as tenesmus, could be a sign of a serious underlying medical condition. When accompanied by rectal pain and bleeding, this most unpleasant sensation can be the first sign of an intestinal inflammation, most commonly a result of either ulcerative colitis or Crohn's disease.

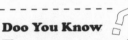

Doo You Know

The average person farts ten times per day, resulting in the release of 705 cc of gas into the atmosphere.

WORLD LEADERS
AND THEIR THRONES

In the late 1600s, King Louis XIV of France regularly held official meetings while sitting on his beloved "throne." Known for his absolute command of power, Louis was an impartial ruler when it came to poo, unabashedly relieving himself in front of royalty and peons alike. Perhaps Louis XIV's comfort level with defecation contributed to his record-setting seventy-two-year reign of power. After all, what opposing ruler could effectively negotiate with the king when faced with the constant threat of having to witness his majesty's next bowel movement?

Three hundred years later, this "open-door" poo policy has been replaced by secrecy and paranoia. On a trip to Vienna, the White House flew in a special presidential crapper so that President George W. Bush's feces could be collected and disposed of in a secure manner. Secret Service agents capture Presidential Poo in order to prevent foreign intelligence agencies from collecting information about the commander in chief's health. Governmental agencies, including the United States' C.I.A. and the Israeli Mossad, have used this approach to gain valuable information on the health status of world leaders such as Mikhail Gorbachev and former Syrian President Hafez al-Assad.

Author Biographies

Josh Richman met his coauthor while they were undergraduates at Brown University, and their shared fascination with the diversity of poo brought them together to write this book. Josh holds an MBA from Stanford University and lives in the San Francisco Bay Area.

Anish Sheth, M.D., holds a medical degree from Brown University, and is currently a gastroenterology fellow at Yale University School of Medicine. He lives in Connecticut with his wife and two-year-old son. Despite his love for poo, Anish is known to frequently disappear when his son's diaper is in need of changing.